Migrant
Music: Jazz

by C.A. Barnhart

Scott Foresman
is an imprint of

Glenview, Illinois • Boston, Massachusetts • Chandler, Arizona
Upper Saddle River, New Jersey

Photographs

Every effort has been made to secure permission and provide appropriate credit for photographic material. The publisher deeply regrets any omission and pledges to correct errors called to its attention in subsequent editions.

Unless otherwise acknowledged, all photographs are the property of Pearson Education, Inc.

Photo locators denoted as follows: Top (T), Center (C), Bottom (B), Left (L), Right (R), Background (Bkgd)

ISBN 13: 978-0-328-52693-2
ISBN 10: 0-328-52693-2

12   16

TABLE OF CONTENTS

Chapter 1
And Then Came Jazz

No one really knows where the word *jazz* came from. However, we have a fairly good idea of where and when jazz, the music, began.

Around 1913, the word *jazz* referred to a kind of dance associated with ragtime. Ragtime music depends on **syncopation**, a rhythmic technique that places emphasis on beats that are usually weak or unaccented. Ragtime started among African American musicians in the late 1890s. Musicologists— scholars who study the development of musical forms—have traced ragtime back to New Orleans. One of its famous composers was Scott Joplin from Missouri. His rags achieved great popularity and were performed in both white and African American dance halls.

Scott Joplin

By the 1930s, *jazz* was the word used to describe the original, **energetic** music that African American musicians wrote and performed. Jazz built upon ragtime. As the popularity of jazz grew, it became recognized as a particularly American musical form. Jazz musicians were admired for their technical and creative musical abilities.

Jazz musicians followed a melody, added notes to it, and changed its rhythm. They were basically creating a new composition every time they played a song. This technique is called **improvisation**.

Jazz became popular in the United States at a time when African Americans and whites lived very separate lives. There was strict separation of the races, yet both races embraced jazz.

Jazz musicians enjoyed great popularity, and some built long and respected careers. More often than not, however, African American performers were not even allowed to **patronize** the very clubs they headlined.

The popularity of jazz did not break down the barriers that kept African Americans out of the mainstream of American life. It did, however, put jazz musicians firmly in the mainstream of American music.

Louis Armstrong is considered one of the greatest of all jazz musicians.

Jazz became popular at a time of strict separation between African Americans and whites.

Chapter 2
Jazz: A Window into the United States

Jazz was the creation of African Americans. In the 1920s, when jazz became a major musical form, the great African American jazz musicians lived segregated lives in the United States. It was not until 1954 that **segregation** in public schools was declared unconstitutional by the U.S. Supreme Court. Segregation was not fully outlawed until the Civil Rights Act passed in 1965. In some ways, the story of jazz has much to do with segregation.

The story of the development of jazz is also one of remarkable and widespread success. In fact, while jazz was new and maturing as a musical form, it was already a powerful cultural force, influencing other forms of music, art, literature, and even language.

Jazz acted somewhat like an American ambassador, especially to European countries. Many Europeans thought of American culture as less refined or less important than their cultures. In the view of Europeans, the United States had not been a country long enough to have established any literary, artistic, or musical traditions.

Like some generalized opinions, these observations about American culture were not necessarily based on facts. The United States had a long tradition of appreciation for the arts, although its artistic expression had been mainly influenced by European traditions. Jazz was something completely different because it was a reflection of American life and had sprung directly from it.

Since the United States was populated by immigrants, American culture was a collection of many, mainly European, cultures. It did not have a particular character of its own—that is, until jazz exploded in night clubs and on concert stages throughout the Americas and Europe. Then jazz became established as a respected and important **genre** of music.

What accounted for the spread of jazz, and who were the people who brought jazz to our nation's musical life? Much of the reason for the spread of jazz lies in the great movement of African American people from one part of the United States to another. These migrations of African Americans, especially from rural areas to urban centers, came about because of economic need. Jazz also spread, however, because African American musicians wanted to be in places where jazz was becoming popular.

Chapter 3
Slavery and Music

To understand the development of jazz, we need to understand the life of African Americans in the United States. Prior to the Civil War, most African American people came to the United States as enslaved people. Not only had they lost their personal freedom, but they were forced to live in a culture with different customs and practices than those they had known. They did not know the language, much less the religion, of their owners.

In expressing their religious beliefs, African Americans blended African and European musical traditions into what we now recognize as African American religious music. This distinct music, made up of spirituals and "sorrow songs," is considered by many musicologists to be a significant part of musical history.

There was another kind of special music made by enslaved people. It included rhythmic sing-song, call-and-response work songs developed by enslaved people working in the fields. Some of the songs were about injustice and hardship. These songs became the basis for the blues, on which jazz is based. The blues is also the source for rhythm and blues, country music, and rock 'n' roll—all of which remain popular today. These work songs did not need any instrument except the voice.

Enslaved people also used the African drumbeat in their songs. Even though it was often illegal to own a drum, they provided a throbbing beat with spoons, dried gourds, and pots. Enslaved workers often provided music for their owners' social occasions.

"Shouts" and "hollers" across the fields were the beginnings of the blues, ragtime, and jazz.

Chapter 4
Two Races, Two Cultures

With the end of slavery after the Civil War, African American life became freer but much less secure. In the South particularly, but actually all over the United States, there were two cultures: white mainstream culture based on European culture, and black African and slave-based culture.

A Civil Rights Act was passed by Congress in 1866, declaring that African Americans were citizens of the United States. The Fourteenth Amendment followed soon after, recognizing their citizenship. Still, African Americans were not treated fairly.

The maintenance of segregation of the races in the South was known as **Jim Crow**. This was a time of great economic and social difficulty for those who had been enslaved. African Americans attended segregated schools and churches.

They ate at separate lunch counters. They found it difficult and sometimes impossible to vote, and it was difficult for them to find good schooling or jobs.

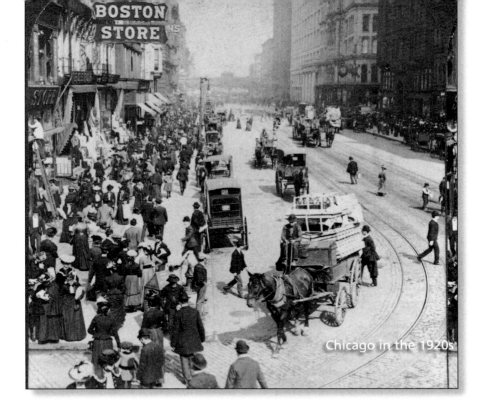
Chicago in the 1920s

Due to the South's strict segregation policies, African Americans reached out to other immigrant groups for both friendship and music. For example, Caribbean Creoles who settled in New Orleans, Louisiana, contributed their unique drumming traditions, as did people from Latin America.

African American people also realized they needed to migrate from the South. Economic opportunities were more plentiful in the fast-growing cities of the North, such as Chicago. This movement brought African American music to other parts of the country.

In both New York and Chicago, where there were audiences with sufficient leisure and money to support jazz, the exciting new music became part of the popular culture. The newly arrived musicians from the South blended with the established musicians in the North, adding more depth and richness to the jazz sound.

11

Chapter 5
Increasing Acceptance

World War I, which raged from 1914 to 1918, helped bring international attention to African American music and musicians. Along with white soldiers, black soldiers joined the armed forces to help our allies fight and win the war. However, African American soldiers were as segregated in the military as they were in civilian life. In spite of this, African Americans distinguished themselves on the battlefield, proving that they were every bit as capable as any other soldiers.

African Americans also distinguished themselves musically during World War I. An army band led by James Reese Europe was made up entirely of African American musicians. It played an original military ragtime march. Commanders saw that the African American band created a mood of friendship wherever it played. African American musicians were gaining important recognition.

After the war, returning African American soldiers found the United States basically unchanged in its attitudes. Segregation still held sway. By the 1920s, shortly after the war, a period of great financial wealth brought great changes to the United States. This time was known as both the Roaring Twenties and the Jazz Age. It marked the solid entry of jazz into American popular culture.

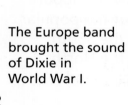

The Europe band brought the sound of Dixie in World War I.

Chapter 6
Growing Appreciation for Jazz

One of the outstanding jazz musicians of this period was Louis Armstrong. He played the cornet and introduced the improvised solo to jazz.

Improvisation is a difficult art and central to jazz. The person who is improvising must have a great musical imagination. An improviser is aware of the structure of the music or the melody line. He or she **embellishes** the music with other sounds that blend well with the original sounds.

Some music critics thought jazz was undisciplined. They did not like its wandering melodies and unpredictable rhythms. However, ordinary people found it wonderfully exciting and free.

The great jazz improvisers became famous, and jazz spread far beyond the United States. The French, in particular, admired jazz and embraced African American jazz musicians. Even classical composers were influenced by jazz. George Gershwin used jazz in his works, *An American in Paris* and *Rhapsody in Blue*.

George Gershwin was a composer who incorporated many jazz elements into his classical compositions.

Louis Armstrong was a successful composer for his jazz band. While in New Orleans, Louis Armstrong was in a successful band called the "Hot Five."

Jacob Lawrence lived and worked in Harlem, home to many African American artists.

During the Jazz Age of the 1920s and beyond, the African American community exploded with many forms of artistic expression. Jacob Lawrence made an extraordinary contribution in visual arts. When asked about influences on his painting, he remarked that he was surrounded by color in Harlem, where he lived. Harlem was home to many African American people and was an important artistic center. The Apollo Theater and the Cotton Club in Harlem attracted huge audiences of both African Americans and whites.

Duke Ellington

Chapter 7
Music and War

Hard economic times followed the Jazz Age of the Roaring Twenties. The Great Depression of the 1930s was a time of financial and emotional loss and distress.

Even so, jazz and jazz-based music in the form of swing music were doing very well. This time, the spread of the new music was not the result of migration, but of radio and recordings. Jazz became international.

Duke Ellington, who became a successful jazz musician in the1920s, went on to become equally successful with his swing band. He was a great pianist and composer. He and his band created an orchestral jazz sound.

During World War II, one million African Americans were in the armed forces. They were again subject to segregation in the army, even though they were risking their lives to save democracy in Europe.

Both black and white entertainers were sent all over the world to bring entertainment to the soldiers. One jazz musician, Artie Shaw, said that all the soldiers wanted to hear was the sound of jazz, which was, for them, the sound of home.

After the war, more African Americans moved to urban areas. This concentration of African Americans in cities energized the musical scene. By the 1950s, another large migration from the Caribbean was bringing new musical traditions to U.S. cities. These Latin musicians brought a different sound and beat. They began to play with American jazz musicians and created yet another version of jazz. Some called it Latin, or Afro-Cuban, jazz.

Dizzie Gillespie

The Beatles

Chapter 8
Jazz Grows Up

The free flow of musical ideas between musicians from different cultures created an exciting musical scene in places such as New York City. Jazz of all kinds was played in clubs all over the city.

Jazz had grown and spread throughout the country as the musicians who played it migrated. Jazz also grew and changed as new musicians from other cultures added their contributions. By the 1960s, other musical influences seemed to overwhelm jazz, especially rock 'n' roll.

The tremendous success of the Beatles, a rock 'n' roll band from England, combined with the influence of television on the genre, hit jazz musicians hard. Many felt as if they had been struck by a thunderbolt. Some turned to rock or rhythm and blues in order to maintain a career. Older jazz musicians wondered if jazz was dead.

Of course, such music does not die. It is claimed and reclaimed by musicians who play it and who develop new sounds and audiences. American jazz, the music that migrated along with the people who developed it, has continued to migrate and adapt. There are internationally recognized jazz musicians all over Europe, the United Kingdom, Latin America, Africa, and Canada. These musicians, like the early jazz musicians, have blended American jazz with their particular musical roots.

In the United States, jazz is regarded as important and serious music. For example, trumpeter Wynton Marsalis began his career in the classical concert hall and is now head of Jazz at Lincoln Center in New York City.

Jazz, whose roots sprouted in the soil of slavery, migrated with musicians from the rural South to become a permanent part of American culture. Jazz is still migrant music, traveling to other cultures just as it was originally spread by its performers in the United States.

Wynton Marsalis

19

Now Try This

After reading *A Migrant Music,* you probably have more questions about jazz and its history. Here are some ways to find out more about the role of jazz in American culture. Break into small groups—perhaps based on interest. Choose one of the following activities and explore more about jazz of yesterday and today. Plan to share your information with the class.

Here's How to Do It!

1. The book does not talk specifically about the role of women in jazz, but there were many famous female jazz performers. There were also many all-female bands that toured during the Depression Era (the 1930s). Here are some names you can investigate: Marjorie Hyams (trumpeter); Elsie Smith (saxophonist); pianists Dolly Adams, Mary Lou Williams, and Emma Barrett; and singers Billie Holiday, Sarah Vaughan, Bessie Smith, and Ethel Waters. See if you can find their recordings or articles about them.

2. The book mentions the role African Americans played in the military during wartime. These men and women contributed to the armed forces and to our victories. Many were medal-winners for their bravery. How much can you find out about their outstanding deeds? After you gather the information, you might wish to create an "honor roll" to remember them.

3. Many young people play in small jazz bands in school. Perhaps you know some students who do, or perhaps you play jazz. You could arrange a mini-jazz festival featuring your fellow students, or you could develop a jazz program for your class. Present recordings of several jazz pieces, and write a program booklet that explains the different jazz selections. Include something about the artists who play the music and something about the jazz artists who made the songs famous.

Glossary

embellishes *v.* makes more interesting by adding details; adorns; decorates.

energetic *adj.* active; vigorous; full of energy.

genre *n.* category; style of art, music, or literature.

improvisation *n.* something that is made up on the spur of the moment.

Jim Crow *n.* systematic discrimination against African Americans.

patronize *v.* to be a regular customer of.

segregation *n.* the separation of one racial group from another.

syncopation *n.* in music, the practice of beginning a tone on an unaccented beat and holding it into an accented one.